Samuel French Acting Edition

Wolf's Blood

by Jethro Compton

Inspired by the novel White Fang *by* Jack London

SAMUELFRENCH.COM   SAMUELFRENCH.CO.UK

Copyright © 2018 by Jethro Compton
Artwork designed by Jethro Compton LTD © 2018 Jethro Compton
All Rights Reserved

WOLF'S BLOOD is fully protected under the copyright laws of the United States of America, the British Commonwealth, including Canada, and all other countries of the Copyright Union. All rights, including professional and amateur stage productions, recitation, lecturing, public reading, motion picture, radio broadcasting, television and the rights of translation into foreign languages are strictly reserved.

ISBN 978-0-573-70727-8

www.SamuelFrench.com
www.SamuelFrench.co.uk

FOR PRODUCTION ENQUIRIES

UNITED STATES AND CANADA
Info@SamuelFrench.com
1-866-598-8449

UNITED KINGDOM AND EUROPE
Plays@SamuelFrench.co.uk
020-7255-4302

Each title is subject to availability from Samuel French, depending upon country of performance. Please be aware that *WOLF'S BLOOD* may not be licensed by Samuel French in your territory. Professional and amateur producers should contact the nearest Samuel French office or licensing partner to verify availability.

CAUTION: Professional and amateur producers are hereby warned that *WOLF'S BLOOD* is subject to a licensing fee. Publication of this play(s) does not imply availability for performance. Both amateurs and professionals considering a production are strongly advised to apply to Samuel French before starting rehearsals, advertising, or booking a theatre. A licensing fee must be paid whether the title(s) is presented for charity or gain and whether or not admission is charged. Professional/Stock licensing fees are quoted upon application to Samuel French.

No one shall make any changes in this title(s) for the purpose of production. No part of this book may be reproduced, stored in a retrieval system, or transmitted in any form, by any means, now known or yet to be invented, including mechanical, electronic, photocopying, recording, videotaping, or otherwise, without the prior written permission of the publisher. No one shall upload this title(s), or part of this title(s), to any social media websites.

For all enquiries regarding motion picture, television, and other media rights, please contact Samuel French.

MUSIC USE NOTE

Licensees are solely responsible for obtaining formal written permission from copyright owners to use copyrighted music in the performance of this play and are strongly cautioned to do so. If no such permission is obtained by the licensee, then the licensee must use only original music that the licensee owns and controls. Licensees are solely responsible and liable for all music clearances and shall indemnify the copyright owners of the play(s) and their licensing agent, Samuel French, against any costs, expenses, losses and liabilities arising from the use of music by licensees. Please contact the appropriate music licensing authority in your territory for the rights to any incidental music.

IMPORTANT BILLING AND CREDIT REQUIREMENTS

If you have obtained performance rights to this title, please refer to your licensing agreement for important billing and credit requirements.

WOLF'S BLOOD was originally presented under the title *WHITE FANG* as a co-production between freeFall Theatre and Jethro Compton Productions with the following creative team:

Director and Set Designer: Jethro Compton

Puppetry Director: James Silson

Associate Director: Ellie Gauge

Original Soundtrack by Jonny Sims

Original Songs by Gavin Whitworth

Original Song Lyrics by Jethro Compton

Original Song Arrangements by Michael Raabe

Costume Designer: Adrin Erra Puente

Lighting Designer: Julian McCready

Sound Designer: Juan Coolio

Puppetry Designer: Eric Davis

Properties Master: Jerid Fox

Musical Director (US): Michael Raabe

Musical Director (UK): Gavin Whitworth

Dramaturgs: Timothy Saunders & Oliver Kassman

Assistant Director (UK): Jessica Knight

Casting Director (UK): Becky Paris

Stage Manager (US): Sarah Smiley

WOLF'S BLOOD had its first performance on September 30, 2017 at freeFall Theatre in St. Petersburg, Florida (Eric Davis, Artistic Director) with the following cast:

LYZBET SCOTT	Jen Diaz
WEEDON SCOTT	Michael Mahoney
CURLY	Hannah Benitez
BEAUTY SMITH	Alan Mohney Jr.
TOM VINCENT	Daniel Schwab
HENRY GRIFFITH	Robert Johnston

WOLF'S BLOOD had its first performance in London on December 14, 2017 at Park Theatre with the following cast:

LYZBET SCOTT	Mariska Ariya
WEEDON SCOTT	Robert G. Slade
CURLY	Bebe Sanders
BEAUTY SMITH	Paul Albertson
TOM VINCENT	Jonathan Mathews
HENRY GRIFFITH	Danny Mahoney

CHARACTERS

LYZBET SCOTT – a young First Nations girl
WEEDON SCOTT – an old huntsman
CURLY – a girl from a nearby homestead
BEAUTY SMITH – a fur trader and businessman from the city
TOM VINCENT – a young hunter
HENRY GRIFFITH – an associate of Beauty Smith
WHITE FANG – a wolf

SETTING

Yukon Territory, Northwest Canada

TIME

1896–1899

AUTHOR'S NOTES

This play began life as an adaptation of Jack London's novel *White Fang*. In fact, the name *Wolf's Blood* comes from the German translation of the story, *Wolfsblut*. My initial ambition was simply to retell the Jack London story from a different perspective – a human perspective.

The lasting impression of the novel was, for me, a struggle for identity. In the novel, this struggle exists within an animal, half-dog, half-wolf, torn between two lives and living in a world occupied by examples of the best and worst of humanity. *Wolf's Blood* sees that struggle take shape within a young woman, born to an indigenous tribe but raised in a white family. I did not set out to write a play about a First Nations character, but as I researched the region of Canada at the time when London's story is set, I discovered a narrative that was, sadly, unknown to me – a part of history I had not been taught and certainly had never seen on stage.

The atrocities committed in the Canadian residential schools, at the hands of Christian churches and the government's Department of Indian Affairs, are something I'd never heard of – and something which seems to be often forgotten in the narrative of the country's past. The more I researched the forced assimilation of Aboriginal Canadian children, the clearer it became to me that I couldn't write a play in that time period, in that location, and ignore the horrific stories I'd read. As I considered the central human character who grew to become the human manifestation of London's wolf, it felt important that this character in some way engage with that dark period of recent history.

Of course, I have to question, and have done throughout this process, what right I have to tell this story. The fear of appropriating another culture's stories, or misrepresenting them, is always present in a writer's mind. However, being in a position of privilege where I was able to share this play with audiences in America and Great Britain, I felt it was far more important to help tell part of the story, than to join with so many who have ignored it for so long.

Note on Puppetry

Despite the fact that White Fang, unlike in London's novel, is not the protagonist of this story, his role is entirely essential to the play and to the human characters within it. Bringing the wolf to life in this story produces a number of unique challenges, but also some fantastic opportunities for moments of impressive and mesmerising storytelling.

In our inaugural production, White Fang was brought to life by three puppets designed by Eric Davis and performed under the puppetry direction of James Silson. The first, an abstract puppet made from elements of firewood that filled the campfire in the prologue. This became known as the "Spirit Wolf," a representation of the character that emerged from the fire's smoke and ran in slow motion through the air, operated by four members of the company.

The second puppet, the "Wolf Pup," was a marionette-style puppet that represented the character in its infancy. With ample movement, under the operation of only the lead puppeteer, the Pup was able to interact with the character of Lyzbet playfully and to great effect. This introduction to the "real-life" White Fang connected the audience to the wolf in its least threatening state – allowing the audience to form a bond with the character before it grew into the leaner, more aggressive wolf.

The third puppet, as described, was the full-size, fierce "Fang." Operated by the lead puppeteer and one supporting puppeteer, Fang moved as a wolf, though never at great speed. He maintained playfulness in his head movements, where he also demonstrated his aggression and power. His physical size allowed him to dominate the stage with his presence, and to provide a realistic threat to other characters.

Noises for the wolf were created by the lead puppeteer who developed growls and whines with great effectiveness. For all moments where we heard Fang's howl we used recorded effects whilst the wolf was unseen by the audience.

The result of all these elements helped create the character of White Fang, but the key tool that brought him to life in the audiences' minds was the way in which the other characters interacted with him. He was, at all times, a living character within his scenes, with thoughts and emotional responses, and those around him never ignored that. Their love for him, their fear of him, was what truly gave him life.

Note on Music

The music for *Wolf's Blood* is required and provided by Samuel French for additional fees.

For my agent, Kelly

ACT ONE

Prologue: Within The Fire's Flame

COMPANY.
THE RIVER FLOWS
WHERE SHADOWS FEAR TO TREAD,
WHERE STARS ARE GONE AND GOD IS DEAD.
IN DARKNESS,
WHERE MOUNTAINS BREAK THE SKY
AND SNOW HAS BURIED ALL THE NIGHT,
I WILL WANDER,
AND THE DARKNESS DEFY,
UNTIL I FIND HIS GUIDING LIGHT.
UNTIL I FIND HIS GUIDING LIGHT.
UNTIL I FIND HIS GUIDING LIGHT.

(At a campfire. An **ELDER** *whittles a scrap of timber to the rough resemblance of a wolf.)*

NARRATION. I've heard a story, whispered in the night, when grey of day has faded into dark and pall of Arctic black has fallen fast. Beneath the spirits' green and swirling light, a girl who gazed within the fire's flame and witnessed there a vision in the smoke – a creature hewn from frost and snow and ice, inside whose gaze, from long before, was life.

(The **ELDER** *lofts the whittled ornament into the pit.)*

(From the flames, a wolf emerges, blackened by the fire's coals.)

(Snow begins to fall. The wind lifts. Battle drums* fill the air.)

(One foot in front of the other, slowly at first, the wolf begins to run. He builds his pace with the pounding drums – faster and faster.)

(He stops, lifts his nose to the moon, and liberates a fearsome howl that carries across the winter air.)

---

*A license to produce *Wolf's Blood* does not include a performance license for any third-party or copyrighted music. Licensees should create an original composition or use music in the public domain. For further information, please see Music Use Note on page 3.

Scene One: The Northland Wild

(The wind batters a tent's faded canvas. Inside is a young man, **TOM VINCENT**. *The penetrating howl reaches his ears, startling him.)*

(Snow lifted on the wind pushes into the tent, escaping the cold night air beyond as an old man, **WEEDON SCOTT**, *wrapped thick in furs, hauls himself inside.)*

TOM. You hear that?

WEEDON. I've got ears.

TOM. They're huntin'!

WEEDON. They're not yodellin'.

TOM. They're closin' in!

WEEDON. How many shots do you have remainin'?

TOM. I dunno.

WEEDON. Count.

TOM. You don't reckon it's gonna come to that?

WEEDON. I reckon those beasts haven't ate for days – maybe longer.

TOM. Three. I got three. Will that be enough?

WEEDON. By my calculation, dependin' on what path you choose to meet your maker, that's a whole two additional.

TOM. It ain't gonna come to that. They ain't gonna get in the tent.

WEEDON. That so? And what 'bout when you need to soil the snow? How you plan on doin' that without presentin' your rear outside?

TOM. I can hold it.

(The pack releases a terrifying howl – surrounding the men.)

WEEDON. You look like you're gonna let it loose every time they yowl.

TOM. I tell you, I can hold it.

WEEDON. How long have you been a hunter, Tom?

TOM. I been a hunter since I was born. My daddy says I come out of my mamma's belly with a forty-eight calibre long rifle in my grip.

WEEDON. No wonder the woman wasn't fond of you. Tell me, Tom, in all those years you've been a hunter – have you ever been hunted?

(Silence.)

When you're the hunter, you got all the time in the universe. Sit. Clutch that rifle. When you're the prey, more often than not, you don't even know you're the prey. So you *believe* you have all the time in the world – till you march right into the hunter's sights; till your leg gets fixed in the snare; till you locate yourself skewered on the sharp end of a spear. That's the hunter's greatest gift, not his proficiency with the blade – time.

(Howls from the wolves. They are closing in.)

The pack have all the time they want. The two of us, we only have the *illusion* of it.

TOM. How many days by foot to Dawson?

WEEDON. Two – if the snow alleviates. Three if it doesn't.

TOM. We can make that. We stick to daylight. And I got three shots. I take down three of 'em, that'll scare the rest of 'em off alright.

(Silence.)

WEEDON. When they come for you, Tom, be certain to stay on your feet.

TOM. They ain't gonna come.

WEEDON. They get you off balance, one of 'em acquires you belly-up, that's when the pack'll move for you.

TOM. They ain't gonna come.

WEEDON. They'll sink their teeth through your neck and be out again before you can reciprocate. They'll let your life flow out your veins. And when they're done with your flesh, they'll eat the crimson snow, and all that'll remain of you will be a morsel of cloth. Even your boots'll be gone. Tough old leather's like prime jerky to a starvin' wolf.

TOM. Why you tellin' me this?

WEEDON. So you know. So you can make the choice before you waste all those bullets.

(Growls come from all around the tent. The pack is close. **WEEDON** *pulls his knife from its sheath.)*

TOM. I ain't ready to die.

WEEDON. What man is?

TOM. I intend to do something with my life. Somethin' significant.

(A wolf is moving closer, growling fiercely.)

WEEDON. Probability is you're soon to provide sustenance for an entire pack of wolves. In the order of life, seems to me there's significance in that.

TOM. You ain't amusin' me.

WEEDON. I intended no amusement. This here is the Northland Wild, son – where we're every one of us animals. The strongest – we hunt, we kill, we survive. Till the day there's a beast stronger. Then we fight. And we die. And the Wild won't shed a tear for our spilt blood. It would freeze before it struck the snow.

(A gunshot pierces the world and couples with the pained yelp of a wounded animal.)

TOM. What in the name of Mother Mary?

(Men's voices can be heard nearby. Sled dogs bark excitedly. A voice comes from outside.)

BEAUTY. *(Offstage.)* Anyone alive in there?

WEEDON. Announce yourself.

BEAUTY. *(Offstage.)* Beauty Smith. Huntin' party out of Grand Forks.

WEEDON. Beauty Smith? Same Beauty Smith tradin' furs down near Whitehorse some years back?

> (**WEEDON** *opens the tent to reveal* **BEAUTY SMITH**, *who steps inside.*)

BEAUTY. Weedon Scott... Well I'll be damned.

WEEDON. This here is Tom Vincent.

BEAUTY. Where are you headed, Weedon?

WEEDON. Three Eagles Mount, east of Dawson.

BEAUTY. The pack had your scent.

WEEDON. I don't believe you're mistaken.

BEAUTY. I trust we've discouraged them for the time being. If they haven't returned to us by then, we intend to pick up their trail first light.

WEEDON. You're out for wolf pelt?

BEAUTY. What about you gentlemen?

WEEDON. Runnin' fur to Broken Ridge.

BEAUTY. On foot?

WEEDON. Lost our sled two days south and made measured progress since.

BEAUTY. You know the score, Weedon, if you can carry your own, you're welcome to join us for the hunt. We'll see you back to Dawson in a day or two, but we don't have time to offer charity.

TOM. We ain't lookin' for charity.

WEEDON. But we'll accept your offer, Beauty. We'll carry our own.

BEAUTY. Alright, gentlemen. Wake yourselves by dawn. We intend to skin those creatures before the sun's full up in the firmament.

NARRATION. By time the sun was down and light was gone, the death had stained the snow its scarlet hue and roughly torn came fur from fallen flesh. But in the midst of bloody painful ends, redemption found small hope in one man's deed. An honest act of pity rarely seen, the creature's years were made a simple gift – one life was saved and so another lived.

Scene Two: In Your Heart

(In a hunter's cabin a young girl, **LYZBET SCOTT**, *is seeing to her chores when the door opens, wind pushing in, carrying the snow.* **WEEDON** *enters.)*

LYZBET. Grandfather! I was expectin' you days ago. Are you well?

WEEDON. I'll be grateful to feel my toes again.

LYZBET. Shall I prepare you somethin'?

WEEDON. Just keep the fire burnin' and bring your grandfather a blanket. Did you go to the settlement?

LYZBET. Yes, sir.

WEEDON. And you secured the trade?

LYZBET. I tried.

WEEDON. You tried?

LYZBET. Yes, sir. But the gentleman at the store –

WEEDON. Perrault?

LYZBET. I attempted the trade, and I explained to him of your bein' absent, but all the same he refused.

WEEDON. It was a good trade.

LYZBET. I know.

WEEDON. You offered it straight?

LYZBET. He wouldn't afford me the opportunity.

WEEDON. On account of what?

LYZBET. On account of me bein' what I am.

WEEDON. On account of your sex?

LYZBET. I figured that was an ingredient of it.

(Silence.)

WEEDON. What did he say?

LYZBET. He made clear he doesn't trade with Indians.

WEEDON. Acquaint me with his precise words.

LYZBET. He informed me he doesn't deal with *savages*.

WEEDON. I ought to ride down there and educate him on what a savage *I* can be.

LYZBET. I'm sorry I couldn't secure the trade, Grandfather.

WEEDON. Now you listen to me, Lyzbet Scott. You listen well and clear. You are never to ask forgiveness from anybody for what you are. Because what you are is nothin' to be ashamed of. You hear me?

LYZBET. Yes, Grandfather.

WEEDON. All that matters is what's in your head and what's in your heart. You understand?

LYZBET. It's just, folk in town look at me different. They look at me like I ain't one of them. Treat me the same way.

WEEDON. Under your skin you're flesh and bone same as all the men and women in that town, even that French sonofabitch Perrault. They don't see it. They *can't* see it. So it's required of you to demonstrate it to them.

LYZBET. But how?

WEEDON. By what's in your head, and what's in your heart. If you're true to those things, in time, they'll learn it. 'Cause the rest of it is nothin' more than meat and bone. And when we're departed from this life, all anyone will recall of us is what we held in head and heart. You understand?

LYZBET. I believe so.

WEEDON. Good. I never want there to be cause to say it again.

LYZBET. Alright.

(Silence.)

WEEDON. You step outside now. You'll discover somethin' out there requirin' attention.

LYZBET. What is it?

WEEDON. I had planned on deliverin' him into town to trade. But it's apparent I've reconsidered. Go take a look. Bring him inside.

*(**LYZBET** steps outside and returns moments later cradling a **WOLF CUB**.)*

LYZBET. Grandfather...

WEEDON. You'll be accountable for him. You'll be liable to feedin' him – trainin' him.

LYZBET. Where's he come from?

WEEDON. He's orphaned. He's too young to survive in the wild and he's requirin' care. If you can't give it, I'll make a sure trade of him.

LYZBET. I'll care for him. You have my word.

WEEDON. That there is a wolf pup, you understand? And in time he'll no longer be a pup. The wolf hasn't been bred out of him, so you'll have to train it out, or beat it out, or you're like to find yourself victim to his bite.

LYZBET. I'll train him. I promise I'll train him well.

WEEDON. That's resolved then.

LYZBET. Thank you, Grandfather.

WEEDON. Alright.

Scene Three: Their Ancient Song

(Through the campfire's smoke we see **LYZBET**, *out in the Northland Wild, training the* **WOLF CUB**.*)*

LYZBET. Sit!

(The **CUB** *doesn't.)*

Sit!

(The **CUB** *doesn't.)*

Koskwâtapi!

(The **CUB** *sits.)*

Kisata...

*(***LYZBET** *slowly backs away. The* **CUB** *follows.)*

Namoya! Namoya! Koskwâtapi...

(The **CUB** *sits.)*

Kisata. Kisata...

*(***LYZBET** *backs away. The* **CUB** *stays.)*

Good boy! Good boy...

(She rushes forward and rewards the **CUB** *with love and cuts of meat.)*

I suppose you're going to need a name.

(Silence.)

Wâpamîpita.

(The **CUB** *responds warmly.)*

Well, I guess that's a yes. Wâpamîpita. It's a good name.

*(***LYZBET** *climbs through the forest and high through the mountains,* **WHITE FANG** *at her side.)*

(Through the fire's smoke, we see **LYZBET**, *sharpening her skill with bow and arrow.)*

(With **FANG** *at her side,* **LYZBET** *grows stronger.)*

NARRATION. The ancient Arctic trees held strong their firs, as white of winter fell in mounting snow, the girl and cub became a single beast and instincts dead awakened from her past. Rememb'ring to a time not long forgot when wild men combed the land and slayed their meat, she quick regained the manner of their skill, with blade and bow and axe she learned the kill – for magic old enthused within her blood. Without endeavor or attempt it came to life as though it had been hers etern. And so as snow had come to pass the year, she lifted eyes toward the watching stars. Ancestors, dead and dust, responded clear, and through the years they called their ancient song – once dead, now in this girl it was reborn.

Scene Four: No Tolerance For Strangers

(Three years later. **WHITE FANG**, *no longer a cub, is by* **LYZBET***'s side. The two are out hunting –* **LYZBET** *is tracking her prey.)*

CURLY. That ain't no regular dog, is it?

(The young girl, **CURLY**, *has snuck up on* **LYZBET**. **FANG** *turns and growls.)*

LYZBET. Namoya! Kisata!

*(***FANG** *stops.)*

He's a wolf. And you'd do well not to approach silent from downwind if you're hopin' to keep your hide intact.

CURLY. I ain't afraid of him.

LYZBET. More fool you. He holds no tolerance for strangers.

CURLY. That right?

LYZBET. Wâpamîpita, kisata.

*(***CURLY** *rifles for something in her pack.)*

You'd be wise to keep your hands where he can see them.

*(***CURLY** *pulls a chunk of meat from a wrapped cloth and offers it out to* **FANG**.*)*

You don't feed another's animal without their blessin'. You hear me?

CURLY. Well, do I get your blessin'?

LYZBET. What's the meat?

CURLY. Rabbit.

LYZBET. He is partial to rabbit.

CURLY. That a yes?

LYZBET. Alright. But don't come complainin' if he takes your hand right along with it. That there's a wild animal.

*(***CURLY** *places the meat down and* **FANG** *approaches slowly.)*

LYZBET. Pêtâ...pêtâ...

    (**FANG** *waits.*)

Michi.

    (*He sniffs the meat and takes a cautious bite.*)

CURLY. He's a *fine* animal – that's for certain. He have a name?

LYZBET. Wâpamîpita.

CURLY. Wapa-what?

LYZBET. Wâpamîpita. It means, White Fang.

CURLY. On account of his white fangs? How imaginative. What the two of you doin' out here?

LYZBET. We were huntin', before you came and kicked up a disturbance.

CURLY. You look like somethin' out of a storybook.

LYZBET. I'm impressed you know how to read.

CURLY. Does it count as readin' if I'm only readin' the pictures? Say...I reckon you're that native lives valley over with Old Man Scott.

LYZBET. Not much gets by you, does it?

CURLY. Is he your daddy?

LYZBET. My grandfather.

CURLY. Then how come you're a redskin?

LYZBET. Perhaps I've been out too long in the sun.

CURLY. You talk strange.

LYZBET. I'd be very satisfied if we weren't talkin' at all.

    (*Silence.*)

CURLY. Everyone calls me Curly.

LYZBET. How nice for everyone.

CURLY. I was born with real curly hair. So they call me Curly.

LYZBET. How imaginative.

CURLY. What about you? You got a native name, or what? Somethin' like "Runs with Bears"? Or "Hunts with Bow"? Or maybe "*Tries* to Hunt with Bow"?

LYZBET. My name is Elizabeth Maria Scott. Named for my grandmother. And if you're keen to find out how well I can hunt with this bow, why don't you start runnin'?

CURLY. Temptin' as that sounds, Elizabeth, don't reckon I have the shoes for it. You ought to be careful out here on your own, Elizabeth. Didn't you hear 'bout that Jim Hall fella? Prisoner 'scaped out of Vancouver?

LYZBET. I can hold my own.

CURLY. Yeah, that was my suspicion.

LYZBET. What about you? You look dressed for walkin' to Sunday prayer, not trudgin' through fresh drift up here in the hills.

CURLY. I can hold my own.

LYZBET. That wasn't *my* suspicion.

(**CURLY** *moves toward* **FANG** *and offers a hand to stroke his fur.*)

You're liable to lose a handful of fingers if you're not wary.

(**FANG** *sniffs around the girl's hand.*)

CURLY. That's a good boy, White Fang. You ain't gonna do me no harm, is you?

LYZBET. You hear me, girl? That there's a wolf. He's not some domesticated lapdog for you to –

(**FANG** *lowers his guard and nuzzles into* **CURLY***'s touch.*)

CURLY. He ain't such a monster.

LYZBET. I've never witnessed him like that with nobody but me.

CURLY. Sure it ain't a personal reflection.

LYZBET. Like I said, he's partial to rabbit. Clear to me you bribed his affections, is all. Come along now, Fang. Sun's fallin' low and I don't intend on returnin' without some meat to show for my troubles.

(**FANG** *hasn't moved.*)

Wâpamîpita! Âstam.

(**FANG** *moves to her.*)

CURLY. Good fortune with your hunt.

LYZBET. You haven't assisted it none. I'll be astounded if there's a creature left in these hills after all your caterwauling.

CURLY. Oh, I'm sure you'll do just fine, Elizabeth.

COMPANY.
THROUGH DEVIL'S GALE AND FEARSOME SWELL
I RIDE THE WAVES TO FIND MY BELLE.
OH THROUGH THE STORM AND THROUGH THE NIGHT
I FIGHT WITH HEART AND GODLY MIGHT.

FOR SHE IS THE GIRL WHO WAITS ON SHORE,
SHE IS THE GIRL THAT I ADORE.

SO I SHALL FIGHT AND I SHAN'T MISS,
BUT IF I DO, REMEMBER THIS,
FOR WHEN I FACE HIS GATES ABOVE,
I FOUGHT WITH HEART AND DIED FOR LOVE.

FOR SHE IS THE GIRL WHO WAITS ON SHORE,
SHE IS THE GIRL THAT I ADORE.

Scene Five: A Good Trade

(In the log cabin, **WEEDON**, **TOM**, **HENRY GRIFFITH**, *and* **BEAUTY** *laugh drunkenly over a bottle of liquor.)*

TOM. Tell me, Beauty, how you got yourself a name like that?

BEAUTY. Isn't it self-evident?

WEEDON. Evidently not.

HENRY. On account of his good looks.

TOM. For real?

BEAUTY. It was a name awarded me in my youth. And one I most respectfully accepted.

TOM. In your youth? By your mamma?

BEAUTY. What's your point, Tom? What point are you making about my mother?

TOM. No. Nothin'...I was just –

BEAUTY. You think my mother seein' beauty in me was on account of her low standards with the rest of the men in her life?

TOM. No! What? I didn't say –

WEEDON. That's what I heard, Tom.

TOM. I didn't say nothin' 'bout no other men.

BEAUTY. Other men? What exactly are you insinuatin', Mr. Vincent?

TOM. What? I ain't insinuatin' nothing!

HENRY. You're insinuatin' his mother was an entertaining girl.

WEEDON. That's exactly what I gleaned from his meaning.

TOM. You're out of your minds!

BEAUTY. So my mother's out for amusement and I'm mentally infirm? Is that what you're sayin'?

TOM. I... No. Weedon, explain I didn't mean nothin' by it.

WEEDON. You dug the grave, you can climb out yourself.

TOM. Mr. Smith, I'm anxious maybe my words fell out wrong –

BEAUTY. You called my mother a whore.

TOM. No. No, I don't believe that I did. Or maybe, if I did, well…well that certainly weren't my intent.

>   (**BEAUTY** *pulls his hunting knife.*)

BEAUTY. Go ahead, Tom. Repeat your accusation.

TOM. Now, there's no cause for that.

BEAUTY. My mother's honor ain't cause?

TOM. That's not… No – Goddamn – You're twistin' my words.

BEAUTY. I ought to cut your tongue out for what you said.

TOM. That ain't necessary… Weedon! Weedon, will you put a stop to this?

WEEDON. I'm afraid this is between the two of you.

>   (**BEAUTY** *grabs* **TOM** *by the jaw and pries open his mouth.* **TOM** *wrestles and cries.*)

BEAUTY. This is the price for insultin' a man's mother.

>   (**BEAUTY** *brings his knife close to* **TOM***'s face, then stops and begins to laugh.*)

Will you look at yourself, Tom? You look about ready to soil yourself.

>   (**WEEDON** *and* **HENRY** *join in laughing.* **WEEDON***'s laugh turns to a vicious cough.*)

TOM. You're havin' me on?

WEEDON. Tom Vincent, you need to either learn to *drink* or learn to drink *less*.

TOM. All of you? You're havin' me on? Goddamn!

BEAUTY. Trust me, Tom, if my mother had been a workin' girl then I wouldn't be sat before you today. I'd have starved to death as a babe on account of her being more unsightly than a gangrenous wound.

>   (*The door opens.* **LYZBET** *steps inside, dead rabbits strung from her belt.*)

WEEDON. I expected you here to prepare lunch.

LYZBET. The game was scarce.

BEAUTY. This must be your granddaughter? I've been hearin' much about you, Miss Scott.

WEEDON. This is Mr. Beauty Smith and his associate, Mr. Henry Griffith.

BEAUTY. A pleasure, Miss Scott.

HENRY. Miss.

TOM. Afternoon, Lyzbet.

WEEDON. These gentlemen are here with a business opportunity. We've made a trade of the eastern ravine.

LYZBET. In exchange for what?

BEAUTY. A small fortune.

LYZBET. Why?

TOM. It was a good trade, Lyzbet.

LYZBET. I'm not askin' you, Tom. Why would we trade that land, Grandfather? That's our land.

WEEDON. No longer.

LYZBET. Why didn't you consult me?

WEEDON. It's my land, Lyzbet, to do with as I please.

LYZBET. I hunt that forest every day.

BEAUTY. And you'll still be welcome to. As my guest.

LYZBET. I won't be a guest on my own land.

WEEDON. Don't forget your manners, girl. Mr. Smith has made a handsome offer.

LYZBET. Has the money transferred hands?

WEEDON. Mr. Smith and I have come to an agreement. The deal is done. So you best wash up, and prepare some food for these men.

LYZBET. You've been drinkin'? How much did you drink before you made the trade? Huh?

WEEDON. You're not too old to feel the back of my hand.

LYZBET. How much did he drink before you made him that offer, Mr. Smith?

BEAUTY. It's a good trade, Lyzbet, but I am never one to cause rupture within a family. I'll withdraw my tender if you fear foul play.

WEEDON. You'll do no such thing! It's more than a fair price you've offered, and I've accepted. Lyzbet, I won't hear another word on the subject. Mr. Smith has been most generous. The coin from this trade will pay for your education for months.

LYZBET. I don't want an education.

WEEDON. You hear the girl? You hear what I'm forced to suffer daily for my act of charity?

LYZBET. I didn't ask for your charity *then*. And I'm not askin' for it *now*. Forego my education and retain the forest. There's more education in those trees than in a hundred schoolbooks.

(Silence.)

WEEDON. You listen to me, Elizabeth. From this day forward, I forbid you from journeyin' east of the ridge. You understand? The eastern woods are off limits. You betray me, and you'll be forbidden from leavin' this house.

LYZBET. But, Grandfather –

WEEDON. I'm tired of you playin' native out in the snow like some overgrown boy. You're a lady – time's come you started actin' like one.

LYZBET. Kiskânak kosisan.

*(**LYZBET** turns and heads outside.)*

WEEDON. Forgive my granddaughter, gentlemen – she has somethin' of a native fire in her.

BEAUTY. She's passionate. It's good for a young lady to have some passion.

WEEDON. Are you overly familiar with the passion of young ladies, Mr. Smith?

HENRY. Not as familiar as he'd like to be.

*(The men laugh and drink. **WEEDON**'s laugh becomes a pained cough.)*

COMPANY.
MY HOMELAND'S CALLING.

MY HEART IS TORN.
AND ALL I LONG FOR,
IS ONCE MORE,

TO SEE MY COUNTRY,
WHERE MY HOME LIES,
ACROSS THE WATERS,
BEYOND THE SKIES.

MY HOMELAND'S CALLING.
MY HEART IS TORN.
AND ALL I LONG FOR,
IS ONCE MORE,

TO SEE MY FAMILY,
TO CROSS THE HEARTH,
OF MY KIN'S HOMESTEAD,
TO BURY MY HEART.

MY HOMELAND'S CALLING.
MY HEART IS TORN.
AND ALL I LONG FOR,
FOREVER MORE,

TO MEET REDEMPTION,
WHERE I WAS BORN.
MY HOMELAND'S CALLING.
MY HEART IS TORN.

Scene Six: Many Kinds Of Respect

(The eastern canyon. **LYZBET** *sings gently as* **WHITE FANG** *comforts her.)*

(Suddenly **FANG**'s *hackles rise. He has caught something on the wind.)*

LYZBET. Keko? Keko? Wâpamîpita? Tânêhki?

*(***FANG** *sets off at a pace.)*

Namoya!

*(***LYZBET** *rushes off after him and moments later they discover a figure collapsed in the snow, huddled under a winter coat.)*

*(***FANG** *whimpers, clawing at the furs. The coat pulls back to reveal* **CURLY**. *She sees the wolf.)*

CURLY. Fang?

LYZBET. Curly?

CURLY. Elizabeth!

LYZBET. Jesus! What's happened to you?

CURLY. You need to get help.

LYZBET. Tell me what's happened.

CURLY. Snow gave way underfoot. My ankle went with it. I reckon it's busted.

LYZBET. Let me take a look.

CURLY. You got eyes can see through skin and flesh? You need to fetch help.

LYZBET. Let me take a look and I'll tell you what I can see.

*(***LYZBET** *examines* **CURLY**'s *leg.)*

How long have you been out here?

CURLY. Few hours – maybe.

LYZBET. You're lucky we found you. Fang got your scent.

CURLY. I knew he liked me.

LYZBET. Your ankle's inflamed somethin' fierce, that's for certain.

CURLY. I could have told you that.

LYZBET. But I don't reckon it's broken.

CURLY. It feels broken.

LYZBET. I can make somethin' to take away the pain – maybe some of the swellin' too.

*(**LYZBET** pulls items from her pack.)*

CURLY. I don't need witchdoctorin', I need you to go back for help.

LYZBET. I won't make it to town and back 'fore dark comes and I don't intend to leave you out here alone through the night. I'll make you somethin' for the pain. Rest it till mornin' – then we'll head for town and get you to Doctor Keenan.

CURLY. What is that?

LYZBET. I don't know it by name. I guess it has one. I just remember it by the leaf. My mother used to call it nipiwin ocepihk – baneroot.

CURLY. Is it safe?

LYZBET. Not everythin' in the wild is lookin' to harm you. There's both good and bad out here, you only need to know where to look for it.

*(**LYZBET** grinds the leaf into a paste.)*

The same leaf, prepared in two different ways – one gives life and the other claims it.

CURLY. Where'd you learn that?

LYZBET. My mother.

CURLY. Your real mother?

LYZBET. Meanin' what, precisely?

CURLY. She was native?

LYZBET. She was.

CURLY. How old were you when you were taken from them?

LYZBET. This will help with the pain.

CURLY. I ain't tryin' to be hurtful. I was just curious, is all.

(Silence.)

LYZBET. I wasn't taken from them. They were taken from me.
CURLY. I'm sorry.
LYZBET. It's likely to burn at first, but that's it doin' its work.
CURLY. I can take it.
LYZBET. Alright.

> (*LYZBET rubs the paste into CURLY's ankle. CURLY silently winces. LYZBET lowers CURLY's leg onto her pack, keeping it raised.*)

That's it. Keep it like that till morning – you'll mark a healthy difference.
CURLY. Thank you.

> (*FANG nestles into CURLY, sensing her suffering.*)

I ain't a princess, you know that? Comparative to you maybe I appear like one. But I ain't. This is my world out here too, you understand?
LYZBET. I didn't say it wasn't.
CURLY. You look at me like this here's my first snow.
LYZBET. I'm not judgin' you.
CURLY. Maybe I don't hunt this land, but I respect it. Maybe in different ways to you, but there are many kinds of respect. I respect the majesty of it.
LYZBET. The majesty?
CURLY. Look at the way the sun's fallin' through them trees, right onto the ice. See up there – see the way the last light is strikin' them mountains, catchin' right in the mist.
LYZBET. Perhaps if you weren't payin' so much attention to its majesty you might have given greater notice to the placement of your feet.
CURLY. Some folk live their whole lives in worlds made of brick and filled with smoke. And other folk live out here, forgettin' just what they should be thankful for every single day.

> (*Silence.*)

LYZBET. If you say so.
CURLY. Everyone's fightin' the land, findin' ways to tame it, to own it – forgettin' to appreciate it for just what it is. Like I said, there are different ways of showin' respect.

   (Silence.)

LYZBET. Is your leg feelin' any better?
CURLY. Mostly it's burnin'.
LYZBET. That's a good sign.
CURLY. Your mother taught you well.
LYZBET. What I can remember of it.
CURLY. I'm sorry, for the time we first met, if what I said upset you.
LYZBET. I don't recall what you said nor bein' upset by it.
CURLY. Just about you bein' a redskin, and all.
LYZBET. No use bein' upset from someone pronouncin' what's true.
CURLY. I guess you must be sick tired of people lookin' at you different – sayin' things.
LYZBET. Can't be tired of hearin' somethin' if you don't listen to it.

   (Silence.)

CURLY. I heard stories, when I was little, that redskins – In'juns – they could move between their human bodies and the animals of the land. Like there was a bond that existed centuries.
LYZBET. Sounds like stories to me.
CURLY. Even so, it's a good story. I always think of it when I make out the eagles hunting over the hills. Often dream of seein' through their eyes, lookin' at the world from up on high. Bet they witness more majesty than we could ever hope for.
LYZBET. You have a lot of words, Curly. But you do put them together nicely.

   *(**CURLY** suddenly leans in and kisses **LYZBET**. **LYZBET** retreats.)*

(Silence.)

LYZBET. I should fetch some wood to build a fire.

CURLY. Alright.

LYZBET. Wâpamîpita, kisata. Kisata.

CURLY. What is that? What are you speakin'?

LYZBET. Fang will stay here with you. He'll watch over you till I return.

NARRATION. By fire's light the power took its hold, restoring wounded hurt beneath her skin. The med'cine was as ancient as the earth, its magic old and wizened by the years, perfected through each soul who'd felt its gift. Where once was cold, where wounded life left ice, now seared a soothing remedy inside, both curse and cure, to warm her through the night.

Scene Seven: Nothing But Trouble

(**LYZBET** *enters the log cabin to find* **TOM** *waiting.*)

TOM. Where you been, Lyzbet? You had us worried keepin' out all night.

LYZBET. I can take care of myself.

TOM. Weedon's been out looking for you – he's fuming. I wouldn't want to be in your shoes right about now.

LYZBET. Well I doubt you'd fill them in any case.

TOM. Why d'you have to fight all the time? Huh? What have I done to you to make you so mad? What's Weedon done? You think you're right the whole time? You think your way's the only way of thinkin'?

(*Silence.*)

You want my advice, Lyzbet?

LYZBET. I guess you're gonna give it either way.

TOM. Show a little respect. Show a little gratitude. Even if you don't feel it – *show* it. 'Cause the way you're goin', you're gonna make enemies of the whole entire world.

(*The door bursts open and* **WEEDON** *storms in.*)

WEEDON. Do you have any idea the grief you've put me through?

LYZBET. I didn't ask for your concern.

WEEDON. You're in my charge, you hear me? When I'm dead you're free to do as you please, but so long as I'm livin' you will do as I say. You understand?

LYZBET. You were drinkin' with your friends and fool me if I thought that would be more essential to you than knowin' my whereabouts. I was of the understandin' that all you cared about was the location of your next bottle.

(*Silence.*)

WEEDON. Tom, get her wolf – and a length of rope.

TOM. Weedon?

WEEDON. Get the wolf and show it in here.

LYZBET. You leave Fang alone.

WEEDON. Bring me that damn wolf.

> (*TOM leaves.*)

LYZBET. If you lay one hand on him –

WEEDON. You're goin' to learn a lesson today, girl.

LYZBET. Why am I the only one who ever needs to learn? Huh?

WEEDON. I am your grandfather. I am a grown man. You understand that? You will do as I say.

> (*TOM opens the door and whistles to* **WHITE FANG**, *who enters cautiously, then sees* **LYZBET** *and bounds across the room to her.* **TOM** *follows in and hands the length of rope to* **WEEDON**.)

> (**WEEDON** *ties a knot in the rope and throws it across the room to* **LYZBET**.)

Pick it up.

> (*Silence.*)

Pick up the rope.

> (*Silence.*)

You make me ask again and I'll come over there and do it for you.

> (*She picks up the rope.*)

Now put it round the wolf's neck.

LYZBET. Grandfather…

WEEDON. Don't question me.

> (*She does it slowly.*)

It's time he was put to use. From now on, he's Tom's responsibility.

LYZBET. No.

WEEDON. From now on he's in with the rest of the dogs. And every time you see him strapped to the sled, I want you to recall the actions that put him there. You understand? Your behavior has done this to him and you can't blame anyone else for that. You need to stop feelin' sorry for yourself and start takin' responsibility. This is how the world works. There are rules and there are consequences for breakin' those rules. You think you're different? Well you're not.

(Silence.)

Tom, take the wolf, put him in the barn with the rest of the dogs.

*(**TOM** slowly approaches **LYZBET**.)*

Hand him over, girl.

(She doesn't.)

Take him, Tom.

(He doesn't.)

Jesus Christ! Will no one in this house do as I say?

*(**WEEDON** storms across the room and grabs the rope and **FANG** by the scruff.)*

LYZBET. Leave him alone!
TOM. Mind yourself!

*(**WEEDON** yells in pain and recoils. He examines his hand. It is bleeding.)*

WEEDON. That sonofabitch!
LYZBET. He was just tryin' to protect me. This isn't his fault.
WEEDON. Like hell it isn't.

*(**FANG** is stood in front of **LYZBET**, growling fiercely, protecting her.)*

He's caused nothin' but trouble. I'll rectify that soon enough.

*(**WEEDON** grabs a shotgun and moves to take aim at **FANG**, who growls violently at the weapon.)*

*(**WEEDON** raises the barrel, but **LYZBET** has moved between the wolf and her grandfather.)*

LYZBET. Stop it! This isn't his fault. He's frightened. He doesn't understand.

WEEDON. I'll make him understand.

LYZBET. No! Please...

WEEDON. It was a mistake saving that cub's life. I should have left it to starve by the corpse of its mother.

LYZBET. Which cub are you talkin' about?

WEEDON. What?

LYZBET. Which cub are you talkin' about? The wolf cub, or me?

*(**WEEDON** lowers the weapon, lost for words.)*

(Silence.)

WEEDON. Get out. Both of you. Get out of my sight.

*(**LYZBET** takes hold of the rope and leads **FANG** outside.)*

You as well. Go on.

*(**TOM** leaves.)*

*(**WEEDON** drops to a stool and begins to quietly cry. He reaches for a bottle and takes a long drink. His cough returns violently – he catches it in his handkerchief.)*

Scene Eight: The Snows Of Winter

NARRATION. The snows of winter cloaked the barren land and buried summer's mem'ries 'neath her mask, a guise of purest white, kept rivers ice, wrecked hope of spring with icy northern winds, and trapped dark secrets firm within her drift. But as the snow and frost and ice held firm, the fire within the girl gave truth the cause, like winter's snow, and winter's ice, to thaw.

> (**LYZBET** *is sitting alone, out among the trees, as* **WHITE FANG** *slowly approaches.*)

LYZBET. Nama, Wâpamîpita.

> (**FANG** *comes closer.*)

Sipwêtê!

> (**LYZBET** *begins to cry. She lowers herself to him and they embrace.*)

Scene Nine: The Great Cause Of Mankind

(**WEEDON** *enters.* **LYZBET** *sits across the room from him, working on a bundle of sticks with her knife, peeling the bark, smoothing and shaping them into arrows for her bow.*)

(**WEEDON** *sits and begins to clean his hunting rifle.*)

WEEDON. I believe we ought to talk.

LYZBET. I have no intention of offerin' an apology.

WEEDON. And I have no desire to fight with you any further.

LYZBET. Is that 'cause the whiskey's worn off and taken your temper with it?

WEEDON. I don't remember when you started speakin' to me like that.

LYZBET. I grew up.

WEEDON. You're still young.

LYZBET. I'm old enough to know the difference between right and wrong. You have no right to bring a man like that into our home.

WEEDON. Our home? I built this house years 'fore you were even born.

LYZBET. And who's taken care of it since? Huh? What's my recompense for all those years of cookin', cleanin', huntin'? All the times I've taken care of you when you're too far in your cups to remove your breeches 'fore you spring a leak.

WEEDON. Don't speak like that.

LYZBET. I am not a little girl.

WEEDON. You're a lady.

LYZBET. I'm more than twice the man Beauty Smith is.

WEEDON. Beauty Smith is a good man!

(**WEEDON** *coughs fiercely.*)

He saved my life – mine and Tom's – three winters past. The deal he's offered for the eastern ravine is more than enough to finance your education. Real money, a real school. The best school. I don't mean in the settlement, I mean the best school in the territory, if they'll take you. And we'll make sure they do.

LYZBET. You mean for me to leave.

WEEDON. I mean to give you a better chance than was ever offered me.

LYZBET. This is my home.

WEEDON. It will still be your home, no matter where you are, this place will always be your home.

LYZBET. Who's gonna take care of it when you can't any longer? Who's going to care for you?

WEEDON. Lyzbet, I understand you can't even picture a world beyond these mountains. But just 'cause you can't picture it doesn't mean it isn't there. It's a big world, filled with danger and excitement. And I have no intention of allowin' you to live out your life tendin' to your grandfather rather'n having the chance to live it.

LYZBET. I have everythin' I need right here. The mountains. The forest. White Fang. You.

WEEDON. White Fang is a wolf. He'll live a few years, then he'll be gone, and so will your opportunity.

LYZBET. What opportunity? To buy my way out of here by portionin' up and sellin' off our land? That forest is our forest. And it's wrong that any man should lay claim to a piece of the earth, but at least we respect it. What's Smith intend to do with that ravine? Fell the trees and dam the river? Destroy what's stood there for centuries for the great cause of mankind's progress?

(Silence.)

WEEDON. I'm dyin', Lyzbet.

LYZBET. What d'you mean you're dyin'?

WEEDON. I mean I'm dyin'. I'm sick.

LYZBET. If you're sick we'll take you to Doctor Keenan.

WEEDON. I've been to Keenan.

LYZBET. When?

WEEDON. Time and time again and every time he tells me the same.

LYZBET. Which is?

WEEDON. He tells me I'm dyin' and there's nothin' to be done about it.

LYZBET. What's the ailment?

WEEDON. Consumption.

LYZBET. There must be medicines can cure it?

WEEDON. There's no medicine.

LYZBET. Maybe not from a white doctor.

WEEDON. Lyzbet, I'm tryin' to be truthful with you. The chances of me witnessin' another summer are remote. The chance of witnessin' the first fall of winter snow, well that's about roughly impossible.

LYZBET. So you're goin' to die?

(Silence.)

Why didn't you say anythin'?

WEEDON. I was hopin' to protect you from it.

LYZBET. I'm sure I might have noticed your death eventually.

WEEDON. I have no intention of leavin' this world knowin' you're here, on your own.

LYZBET. I'm never alone – not here. Here I have everything and everyone I could need. You send me away, to the city – *then* I'll be alone.

WEEDON. I'm tryin' to do what's best for you.

LYZBET. Let me decide what's best.

WEEDON. You're just a child.

LYZBET. You see me as a child because when you look at me you still see that little girl, standin' in that clearin' in the midst of all them bodies. You saved me then. Sendin' me away now will just have postponed the anguish.

(Silence.)

Grandfather. This is my home. This is the land my people occupied for centuries. This land, my tie with it, it's all I have left of them. Can't you understand? If you send me away, every trace of their memory will be washed from me.

(Silence.)

*(**WEEDON** slowly rises and moves to an old trunk. He opens it and rummages through its contents.)*

WEEDON. I told myself to burn this long ago. I couldn't bring myself to do it.

(He shows her an old garment of clothing.)

You were bare when I found you. I wrapped you in this.

(He hands her the garment.)

LYZBET. My mother's?

WEEDON. I don't know.

LYZBET. Thank you. Thank you, Grandfather.

(Silence.)

WEEDON. I drink to alleviate the pain. But I know it's brought a great distance between us. That gives me more hurt than the pain which I'd hoped to drown. Maybe you'll not find forgiveness, but I truly hope you'll find some understandin'.

*(**WEEDON** pulls his coat over his shoulders and walks out into the snow.)*

COMPANY.
OH HEAR THIS VERSE, MY BURDEN'S SONG,
A CALLING TO THE LORD ON HIGH.
FOR OF THIS WORLD, I'M BOUND TO SAIL,
AND FROM THIS FLEETING LIFE I'LL RISE.

CARRY ME, THAT I SHALL NOT FALL FROM HIS GRACE.
OH CARRY ME, 'PON SOARING WINGS OF LOVE.
CARRY ME, THAT I SHALL WITH HIS LOVE BE SAVED.
OH CARRY ME, FOR HIS SALVATION LIES ABOVE.

Scene Ten: Sacred Land

(**WEEDON** *is sat alone in the cabin. The dogs bark outside before a heavy knock comes at the door.*)

(**BEAUTY** *pushes open the door and steps inside. He is accompanied by* **HENRY**.)

BEAUTY. Good evenin', Weedon.

WEEDON. Beauty. Mr. Griffith.

HENRY. Evenin'.

WEEDON. What brings you gentlemen out here so late?

BEAUTY. Business, I'm afraid to say.

WEEDON. What business?

BEAUTY. We have secured an investor – a private benefactor who is keen to support our business venture in these hills.

WEEDON. Go on.

BEAUTY. He departs for Fort Yukon tomorrow morning and he won't be in this direction again until the worst of winter has gone. The stipulation of his financial input is witnessing in person the title deeds to the various parcels of land I have secured.

WEEDON. I'm tired, Beauty – will you arrive at the point.

(**BEAUTY** *pulls a contract from his pack.*)

BEAUTY. With your ink on this document we will secure the funding and we will deliver our agreed sum to you before the end of the week.

WEEDON. I understand.

BEAUTY. Excellent. So, Weedon, we had a gentlemen's indenture, the moment's come we endorse it.

WEEDON. I'm afraid I'm goin' to need some time to consider.

BEAUTY. Time is not available to us, Weedon. I was of the understanding we had agreed the terms?

WEEDON. The situation has become complicated.

BEAUTY. Without this deed I will lose the support of my financier. Without my financier's support I will have no means to uphold our agreement.

WEEDON. If you lack the means, and I the inclination, perhaps that might be the best course for us both.

BEAUTY. I do not lack the means, but if you cause unnecessary delay you shall remove those means from me. Do you understand?

(Silence.)

What is the complication?

WEEDON. My granddaughter.

BEAUTY. She is an impetuous girl who has too much of the savage in her blood. Trust me, Weedon, once we have furnished her purse with silver she will arrive happily at the required way of thinking.

(Silence.)

WEEDON. What do you intend with the land?

BEAUTY. What matter is it?

WEEDON. It's significant.

BEAUTY. The river will provide my company swift access.

WEEDON. Access to what?

BEAUTY. To my proposed mine in the Black Rock Hills.

WEEDON. That's Indian land.

BEAUTY. It was. Now it belongs to me.

WEEDON. That's sacred land.

BEAUTY. So I have heard. Amazing coincidence the way savages declare land sacred the moment a white man discovers gold beneath it.

(Silence.)

WEEDON. I consider myself a man of my word, nonetheless, regretfully, I cannot honor our previous indenture. Forgive me, Beauty. I won't sign the deed. Not tonight. Nor tomorrow. Never.

(Silence.)

BEAUTY. Shall we have a drink, Weedon?

WEEDON. Whiskey won't encourage me to sign.

BEAUTY. I've no intention of coercing a drunken signature.

WEEDON. Beauty, I've made my decision and I won't be moved from it.

BEAUTY. I can see you are resolute. That's no reason we can't share a drink.

WEEDON. Of course.

*(**WEEDON** retrieves a bottle and glasses.)*

BEAUTY. Where is your lovely granddaughter this evening?

WEEDON. I'd suggest she's out huntin'.

BEAUTY. And our good friend, young Tom?

WEEDON. Into Three Eagles.

BEAUTY. A fine shame they won't be able to join us for this drink.

*(**WEEDON** pours the drinks.)*

HENRY. I seen your granddaughter about. On my visit 'fore.

WEEDON. What of it?

HENRY. That wolf. It's a powerful lookin' beast.

WEEDON. That it is.

HENRY. You put that wolf in the pit against a regular hound, you'd make some good coin.

WEEDON. Dog fightin'?

HENRY. I made good coin over in Fort Yukon pittin' mutts 'gainst each other. You get one, a fighter, you make more coin than runnin' whores. Now that's for a reg'lar fightin' dog. With a wolf, now – a wolf, that ain't no reg'lar fightin' dog. Dogs – reg'lar fightin' dogs – got most the bite bred out of 'em. But wolf is full killer. A wolf ain't no reg'lar fightin' dog. Got murder in its blood. Beast like your little girly's wolf – he'd make good coin in no time. You think about this. Give that wolf to me. I train it. I pit it 'gainst the reg'lar fightin' dogs in Fort Yukon. I share the rewards with you.

WEEDON. I don't think so, Mr. Griffith.

HENRY. Shame. That ain't no reg'lar fightin' dog.

BEAUTY. Well, gentlemen. Let's toast. In some form, a conclusion of our business.

WEEDON. Without animosity?

BEAUTY. A conclusion of our business. Without animosity.

(They drink.)

COMPANY.
CARRY ME, THAT I SHALL NOT FALL FROM HIS GRACE.
CARRY ME 'PON SOARING WINGS OF LOVE.
CARRY ME, THAT I SHALL WITH HIS LOVE BE SAVED.
OH CARRY ME, FOR SALVATION LIES ABOVE.

Scene Eleven: The Spirit Crow

*(In the wilderness, **LYZBET** sits by a campfire with **WHITE FANG**.)*

LYZBET. When I was a child, there was a story the elders told around the fire. I heard it a thousand times. They talked of a spirit crow that lived in the mountains. They say he created the land, the sky, and everythin' between. But, like all nature, like all the crow had created, he contained both good and evil. And for his evil, his feathers were painted black for the rest of eternity. So no matter how much light he brings, his black coat is inescapable and he will only ever be seen for his wickedness.

*(**FANG** nuzzles into her.)*

What do you think, Fang?

(He looks at her.)

D'you think Grandfather's right? D'you think I should leave this place? Go south and get an education?

(He looks more closely at her.)

Maybe he is right. Maybe he won't be around forever. And neither will you. Maybe it's time for me to grow up. What do you think? Huh?

(A wolf howls in the very distance.)

*(**FANG** and **LYZBET** jump to their feet, looking off into the darkness.)*

(Then another howl, closer.)

Grandfather...

(Then another, closer still.)

Niyâ! Kiwe!

*(**FANG** charges off into the night.)*

(All around, the stillness of the night has filled with the haunting cry.)

Scene Twelve: The Meaning Of Fear

*(**WHITE FANG** pushes open the door into the cabin. His hackles rise. He growls and sniffs about the room.)*

*(**LYZBET** bursts in. She sees **WEEDON**, slumped at the table. She rushes to him.)*

LYZBET. Grandfather?

*(**FANG** watches from a distance.)*

*(**LYZBET** puts a hand on **WEEDON**, searching for life. Nothing.)*

(She finds the wound – her hands covered in his blood.)

(She slowly lowers herself to the ground in shock.)

*(**FANG** approaches her and offers comfort. **LYZBET** recoils.)*

(A noise outside startles them.)

*(**FANG** moves forward, ready to fight.)*

*(**TOM** bursts in through the door.)*

TOM. Lyzbet? Lyzbet! What in the hell?

*(**TOM** sees **WEEDON**'s body.)*

What's happened?

LYZBET. He's dead.

TOM. Jesus Christ...

LYZBET. It's murder.

TOM. Were you here? You see the man who done it?

*(**LYZBET** shakes her head.)*

Jim Hall's been sighted near the settlement.

*(**LYZBET** doesn't know what he's talking about.)*

Jim Hall. The 'scaped convict. The fella with his face on every wanted poster in town. He was seen headed out this way. We tried to get here fast as we could. We tried to warn you both.

> *(Silence.)*

LYZBET. Who's "we"?

> *(A noise outside. The door opens and **BEAUTY** enters.)*
>
> *(**BEAUTY** looks to **WEEDON**'s body and to **LYZBET**.)*
>
> *(**FANG** growls slowly.)*

BEAUTY. I'm so terribly sorry, Miss Scott. We came here as fast as we could. As soon as I heard the news of the sighting, I went straight to Tom and we travelled as fast as our horses would carry us. May God forgive us we weren't fast enough.

> *(**LYZBET** goes to her grandfather's body. She lowers herself beside him and begins to sob.)*

You're grieving, Miss Scott. You're in shock. Let me escort you to the settlement. We'll take you to see the physician. And we'll speak to the law immediately. I'll have this taken care of.

> *(Silence.)*

TOM. Ain't somethin' missin'?

BEAUTY. Such as?

TOM. I mean, ain't nothin' been taken? Jim Hall come through here – what for? For murder? Why'd he want the law fresh on 'im?

BEAUTY. I don't follow you, Tom.

TOM. I mean, he's come out here and killed a man and what's he got for his troubles? Nothin' more than blood on his hands and a posse on his tail. I mean, why didn't he rob nothin'?

> *(Silence.)*

BEAUTY. Have you checked the barn?

TOM. What?

BEAUTY. Have you checked the barn?

TOM. Oh my God...

(TOM rushes out.)

BEAUTY. Jim Hall will hang for this. I give you my word, Miss Scott. He will face justice for this. And he *will* hang.

(Silence.)

Your grandfather was a dear friend to me. I admired him greatly.

(LYZBET doesn't react.)

You should come away from him now. It's not right for you to see him like this. It's not right a girl should see something so terrible.

LYZBET. You've got no place here, Mr. Smith.

BEAUTY. I beg your pardon?

LYZBET. You're not one of us. You don't belong here. You should leave.

BEAUTY. Of course. As you wish, Lyzbet. I'll leave you to mourn. You send Tom for me if you should need anything. Your grandfather was my friend – I should like to do right by you, as he would have wished.

(TOM rushes in.)

TOM. He's taken the dogs. Sled too.

(LYZBET thinks. She looks to the men, then jumps into action and starts to throw items into her pack.)

BEAUTY. What are you going to do, Miss Scott?

LYZBET. The sled will cut a trail right through the snow. I'm goin' to follow that trail. And I'm goin' to find Jim Hall.

TOM. Rushin' out after him ain't gonna do you no good.

BEAUTY. Tom's right. You need to calm down. You're in shock. Please, Lyzbet –

(He tries to put a comforting hand on her.)

(She pushes him against the wall, pulling her hunting knife to his throat.)

*(**FANG** moves to join the attack.)*

LYZBET. Pêtâ, Wâpamîpita.

*(**FANG** pauses, still ready to fight.)*

If you touch me – if you come near me, near my family again – I won't hesitate to carve you ear to ear. Am I understood?

TOM. Lyzbet! What in the hell you doin'? The man's only tryin' to help.

LYZBET. Am I understood?

BEAUTY. Perfectly.

(She releases him.)

LYZBET. Then get out.

*(**BEAUTY** composes himself and heads toward the door. He leaves.)*

TOM. He was only tryin' to help. You didn't need to behave like that.

LYZBET. Tom, I intend to head out in that snow and find my grandfather's killer. Either aid me in that cause, or don't. But either way, I'm not interested in your advice regardin' my social niceties.

TOM. Lyzbet, wait till mornin'. Wait till there's light to see by.

LYZBET. Jim Hall won't be waitin'. He'll be runnin'. And so long as he's runnin', so will I.

TOM. What 'bout your grandfather?

LYZBET. What about him?

TOM. You can't leave him like this.

LYZBET. Dig a grave – out on the mount.

TOM. You ain't gonna stay to pay your respects?

LYZBET. No, I'm gonna go. And I'm gonna pay him the greatest respect – by killin' the man who put him in that grave.

TOM. Lyzbet, this is sheer foolishness. How d'you intend to catch him? Even if you can track him, you can't keep pace with the sled.

LYZBET. I'll keep pace alright. Fang will go with me – and this won't be the first time we've hunted together. That is *our* forest. These are *our* mountains. This is *our* land. And as long as Jim Hall runs his steps within our snow, and breathes our air, he'll find no sanctuary. Now I guess a man like Jim Hall isn't afraid of much. Least of all a little girl. But by the time I've hunted him, I guarantee you, he will know the meanin' of fear.

*(***LYZBET*** swings her pack over her shoulder.)*

Wâpamîpita, machi.

(She heads out the door, with **WHITE FANG** *by her side.)*

End of Act One

ACT TWO

Scene One: Red Stain In The Snow

COMPANY.
>THE RIVER FLOWS
>WHERE SHADOWS FEAR TO TREAD,
>WHERE STARS ARE GONE AND GOD IS DEAD.
>IN DARKNESS,
>WHERE MOUNTAINS BREAK THE SKY
>AND SNOW HAS BURIED ALL THE NIGHT,
>I WILL WANDER,
>AND THE DARKNESS DEFY,
>UNTIL I FIND HIS GUIDING LIGHT.
>UNTIL I FIND HIS GUIDING LIGHT.

NARRATION. Now through the hostile sleet and heavy snow, the girl and wolf become a single strength, their snowdrift tracks composing vengeful song – poetic verse of huntress and her prey. And on the mountain's face she spies his torch, a gory scratch within a skin of white, as hour arrives to pay that which he owes. Her vengeance now red-written in the snow.

>*(Outside the tent a storm is raging.* **HENRY** *is huddled beneath thick furs – drinking whiskey.)*

>*(The dogs start to bark outside.)*

HENRY. Goddamn those beasts! Keep quiet you filthy mongrels!

>*(They continue to bark.)*

Jesus!

*(**HENRY** wraps himself in his coat, collects a whip, and heads out.)*

HENRY. *(Offstage.)* Quit it!

(The crack of a whip precedes the yelp of a hound.)

(Offstage.) That's enough, you hear me?

*(The dogs are quiet. **HENRY** returns to the tent.)*

(He hurriedly swigs whiskey and wraps furs tight around him.)

(The dogs start to bark again. More excitedly this time.)

Goddamn it! I'll give 'em somethin' to yell about.

(He throws off the furs and pulls open the tent flaps.)

(A spray of red.)

*(**HENRY** is clutching his throat, spluttering, coughing, choking on his own blood.)*

*(Dripping knife in her hand, **LYZBET** moves into the tent. The mist of blood across her face.)*

*(**WHITE FANG** walks in beside her, his head low, ready to pounce if needed.)*

*(**LYZBET** stands over **HENRY**. His hand fumbles for the revolver in his pack. He lifts it toward her, but she pulls it calmly from his fingers. She sits, watching him die.)*

LYZBET. You have my grandfather to thank for your swift end. He taught me to hunt with respect – to take the kill without causin' unrequired sufferin'. The past days I've hunted you, I've thought over and again on what pain I'd wish to bestow upon you. In truth, I should have gone for the heart. But then we wouldn't be here havin' this conversation. And it was significant to me, that you die knowin' on whose blade. The old man at Three Eagles Mount. That man was my grandfather. You spilled his blood. Now I've spilled yours. The discrepancy bein' that his blood leaves its mark on this world. He'll be remembered for what was in his heart. No one will remember you. You'll just be a corpse, lost out here in the storm. A meal for wolves and bears. A red stain in the snow. And no one will shed a tear for the conclusion of Jim Hall.

*(**HENRY** shakes his head, trying to speak.)*

Close your eyes, Jim. Your life's finished – you may as well let it go.

(He tries to speak. Blood spills from his lips. He becomes motionless.)

*(**LYZBET** moves to him. She checks. He is dead.)*

Wâpamîpita. Michi.

*(**FANG** lets out a long, triumphant howl.)*

Scene Two: The Coal Of His Feathers

(In the cabin, CURLY and TOM are sitting by the fire, trying to keep warm. Outside the storm is raging.)

TOM. I don't see no point in you waitin' no longer. It ain't doin' no one no good.

CURLY. I want to be here for when she returns.

TOM. We ain't got no clue when that might be. For all we know she might never return.

CURLY. She'll return.

TOM. Regard the facts, miss, she's been gone days. Out there in the wild – alone. She's a little girl.

CURLY. She'll return. I know she will.

TOM. You know? You know what's out there? Wolves. Bears. Ice. Snow. This ain't a storybook – men die out there. Real men. Strong men. How does a little girl stand a chance in hell?

CURLY. We just gotta keep hope.

TOM. You know what her grandfather would say to that? Hope in somethin' hopeless ain't hope, it's idiocy.

CURLY. Nothin's hopeless till you decide it is. Sure there's danger out there. There's danger everywhere in this world. But there's good as well. You just need to know where to look for it. You know who taught me that? Elizabeth did. So I'm waitin' here for her return. If you've given up hope of that, then maybe you're the one ought to leave.

TOM. I don't have nowhere to go.

CURLY. Then quit thinkin' such thoughts. Nothin' good never came from thoughts like that.

TOM. I can see why Lyzbet likes you. Two of you cut from the same cloth. And that ain't necessarily meant as a compliment.

CURLY. Well I'm takin' it as one.

(Silence.)

How'd she come to live here – with the old man?

TOM. She ain't never told you?

CURLY. No.

TOM. How d'you come to know Lyzbet? She ain't never mentioned you.

CURLY. We're friends.

TOM. Seems strange to me you turnin' up here.

CURLY. Seems strange to me you won't answer my question.

TOM. There was a fight 'tween a group of wolfers and a native tribe. Well, not much of a fight, I guess. Wolfers slaughtered them over some disagreement. A lot of folk died, includin' Lyzbet's mamma and papa. Weedon rescued her, brought her back here and that's about the end of it.

CURLY. Where was this?

TOM. A long ways from here.

CURLY. And what was Weedon doin' there?

TOM. I never asked.

CURLY. Lucky he found her.

TOM. That she was.

(Dogs bark, barely heard over the storm.)

CURLY. You hear that?

(The barks are closer.)

(The door bursts open. Snow pours into the room. LYZBET almost falls inside.)

Elizabeth?

TOM. Jesus Christ!

(They rush to her and pull her in by the fire.)

CURLY. Are you alright? Are you hurt?

TOM. We need to call for the doctor.

LYZBET. No, I'm…I'm alright.

TOM. The hell you are.

LYZBET. The blizzard – cut me off. Fang's on the sled. He needs help.

CURLY. We'll get to him. First we need to get you warm.

LYZBET. No, go tend to Fang.

> (**CURLY** *has removed* **LYZBET**'s *gloves. The fingers are black.*)

CURLY. Oh Jesus...

TOM. What is it?

CURLY. Frostbite. Tom, get Fang into the barn. Then make for Three Eagles.

TOM. We need to get her to the doctor.

CURLY. We ain't takin' her back out into the cold. You bring the doctor here.

TOM. Time he's here there won't be nothin' he can do to save them fingers. You know that well as I do!

LYZBET. I'm not losin' 'em...

CURLY. Damn right you ain't. Tom, get the doctor. I'll do what I can till then.

TOM. I'll go fast as I can.

> (**TOM** *rushes out.*)
>
> (**CURLY** *opens a pack and pulls out some leaves and begins to grind them with the butt of a knife.*)

CURLY. You're gonna be alright, Elizabeth. You hear me? You're gonna be just fine.

> (**LYZBET**'s *eyes are falling shut.*)

We're gonna get you through this. You hear me? Tell me you're gonna survive.

LYZBET. I'm gonna survive...

CURLY. You're the goddamn strongest person I ever met. You know that? You're fearsome strong. You're a survivor. I ever told you that?

> (**CURLY** *moves back to* **LYZBET** *and starts removing her furs and outer layers.*)
>
> (*She pulls a blanket and wraps it round* **LYZBET**, *then begins to apply the paste to her frostbitten fingers.*)

You see this? This is gonna take away the pain. This is gonna heal you somethin' serious. You understand? You ain't losin' no fingers and you for certain ain't gonna die today. You hear me, girl?

LYZBET. He's dead…

CURLY. Who's dead?

LYZBET. Jim Hall…

CURLY. You did good, Elizabeth. You did real good.

LYZBET. I'm cold…

CURLY. I know. I got you now.

(**CURLY** *sits with her by the fire, holding her.*)

LYZBET. They painted him black. But he isn't all evil. There's light inside him also.

CURLY. What are you talkin' about? You're burnin' up.

LYZBET. I saw him.

CURLY. Saw who?

LYZBET. The crow. I saw him. In the blizzard. Dogs had lost the track.

CURLY. Alright. You try and rest some.

LYZBET. But the crow. He was there. The whole world turned white 'cept for the coal of his feathers. And Fang saw him. Fang followed him. Followed him right over the mountains and he wouldn't stop.

CURLY. He's gonna be alright, Lyzbet. You're safe now. I've got hold of you. I got hold of you and I ain't lettin' go. So you just close your eyes. This storm's gonna pass and everythin' is gonna be just fine.

NARRATION. The season's war still waged without a truce, though, true, the worst of winter's storm moved on, but left behind a bitter frozen scar, a frostbit blackened kiss on freezing lips, a glacial blade, an icy Arctic sword stuck deep within the flesh of all she touched, not least where death had cruelly marked the snow. In lupine heart lodged dagger firm and true, so cutting there a second heart in two.

Scene Three: She Taught The Both Of Us

>   (**LYZBET** *is lying in the cabin, wrapped in blankets by the fire. The storm has passed.*)
>
>   (**CURLY** *enters from outside.* **LYZBET** *barely wakes.*)

LYZBET. Curly? Is that you?

CURLY. Well, hey there.

LYZBET. How long have I been out?

CURLY. Few days. How you feelin' for it?

LYZBET. Tired. What are you doin' here?

CURLY. Just tryin' to help, is all.

LYZBET. Why would you help me?

CURLY. Figured I owed you – that night you found me out in the snow. Heard the news in town, 'bout your grandpa, and figured I'd come make myself of use.

LYZBET. You've been here this entire time?

CURLY. Figured it was the least I could do.

LYZBET. You've taken care of me this entire time?

CURLY. Tom's been helpin'.

LYZBET. Where is he?

CURLY. Joined a huntin' party headed out east – two days back.

LYZBET. You didn't have to stay.

CURLY. You ain't grateful?

LYZBET. You know I am. I'm just sayin', you didn't have to.

CURLY. Of course I did. How's them fingers feelin'?

LYZBET. Brand new.

CURLY. The doctor out of Three Eagles fully intended to remove 'em for you.

LYZBET. Well I'm relieved he didn't. What made him change his mind?

CURLY. He didn't change his mind. I just informed him if he amputated any of your extremities I'd be certain to amputate one or two of his. Anyhow, I figured you'd be more inclined for some good old-fashioned witchdoctorin'.

LYZBET. You made up the poultice.

CURLY. Just like you showed me. Like I've said, your mother taught you well.

LYZBET. I guess now she's taught the both of us.

(Silence.)

Where's White Fang?

(Silence.)

Curly? Where's Fang?

CURLY. I'm sorry, Elizabeth...

LYZBET. What is it?

CURLY. He ain't doin' so well.

LYZBET. Tell me.

CURLY. He ain't barely moved since we got him to the barn. It's like he's given up the will. Tom reckons he's dying. I don't disagree.

LYZBET. I want to see him.

CURLY. You ain't strong enough.

LYZBET. The hell I'm not. I want to see him.

(She tries to get up, but her legs can barely hold her.)

Help me.

CURLY. This is madness, you need to rest. There ain't no use in you gettin' sicker and there's nothin' you can do for him.

LYZBET. You either help me to the barn, or you get out and you don't come back.

*(**CURLY** moves to **LYZBET** and helps her up.)*

Scene Four: Not For Anything But Love

*(In the barn, **WHITE FANG** lies almost motionless. **CURLY** helps **LYZBET** to his side.)*

LYZBET. Wâpamîpita...

(The wolf barely lifts his head. His breathing is slow and labored.)

You're gonna be alright. Aren't you, boy?

CURLY. He's lookin' worse by the minute. I'm sorry.

LYZBET. You ran too hard. Didn't you? I shouldn't have let you. That run was too hard for anyone to survive.

CURLY. I'm certain you didn't let him. I'm certain he would have done it with or without your blessin'. 'Cause you'd have died out there without him and he knew it.

LYZBET. You hear that, Fang? Curly reckons you saved me. What d'you think of that? Huh?

(Silence.)

You can't do somethin' so brave, somethin' so selfless and then just give up on livin'. You hear me? I won't allow it.

CURLY. Lyzbet, his breathin's real slow.

LYZBET. *(To* **FANG**.*)* You never gave up on me. I'm not givin' up on you.

CURLY. He's goin' to die, Elizabeth. We both know that. Look in his eyes – he knows it too.

LYZBET. *(To* **FANG**.*)* You can fight it, can't you, boy? We can fight it together.

CURLY. I'm sorry. You know I'm sorry. But he is goin' to die. So you can either pretend like he ain't and waste the time you have left with him, or you can use that time and you can make your farewells. By rights he should have gone days ago. But he's here. He's here and I reckon he's here to see that you're safe. So you tell him you're safe. You tell him you love him. And you give him permission.

(Silence.)

LYZBET. Permission?

CURLY. To close his eyes. To rest. Give him permission to go.

LYZBET. I can't.

CURLY. You can.

(Silence.)

*(**FANG** is barely breathing.)*

LYZBET. This wolf is the strongest creature I've ever met.

CURLY. The two of you were lucky you found each other.

LYZBET. I reckon I'm the lucky one.

CURLY. Lord knows what variety of life he'd have led out there in the wild.

LYZBET. But I would never have asked him to give it up to save me.

CURLY. You didn't ask. This here was his choice; you know that well as I. He made his choice, and he made it not for anythin' but love – his love for you.

*(**LYZBET** turns to **FANG**.)*

LYZBET. *(To **FANG**.)* You're tired – aren't you?

*(**FANG** barely lifts his head to her.)*

It's alright. You rest. You rest now. It's alright. I'm here. I'm not goin' anywhere. You sleep. You close your eyes. You go to sleep now, boy. It's alright.

*(**FANG** is still.)*

*(**LYZBET** lays a hand on him as tears run down her face.)*

(Silence.)

(She covers him with a blanket.)

Kîhtwâm ka-wâpamitin, Wâpamîpita. Kîhtwâm ka-wâpamitin, nîtotêm.

*(Later, in the light of a roaring fire, **LYZBET** carries **WHITE FANG**'s body to the flames.)*

Scene Five: Something Worth Fighting For

(**LYZBET** *is alone inside the cabin when a knock comes at the door.*)

BEAUTY. *(Offstage.)* Lyzbet? Are you in there?

(*He enters.*)

LYZBET. What do you want, Mr. Smith?

BEAUTY. I heard the news of your wolf. Another tragedy. Though I'm relieved to see your health has recovered.

LYZBET. My patience hasn't.

BEAUTY. Then I'll hasten to the point. I wish to do right by you, Miss Scott.

LYZBET. I don't want your money, Mr. Smith.

BEAUTY. And I'm not offerin' it. But I have made arrangements to see your grandfather's wishes be met.

LYZBET. What wishes?

BEAUTY. Weedon made clear to me his intent for you to receive an education. And, fortunately, I have an acquaintance well positioned within the Department of Indian Affairs. Arrangements have been made. I'm to deliver you to Dawson as soon as your health has recovered enough for travel.

LYZBET. The Department of Indian Affairs?

BEAUTY. I'm sure you've heard stories, Lyzbet. But that's exactly what they are – stories. Your people are good at tellin' them. That doesn't make them true.

LYZBET. I'm not your ward.

BEAUTY. Then you'll soon become a ward of the state.

LYZBET. I can take care of myself.

BEAUTY. How? By what means will you survive?

LYZBET. I'll continue my grandfather's work.

BEAUTY. And who will trade with you?

(*Silence.*)

I'm tryin' to help, Lyzbet. The arrangements have been made.

LYZBET. Then please unmake them.

BEAUTY. I'm afraid that's not possible. You're registered with the department. They're expectin' you.

LYZBET. I won't go.

BEAUTY. You must.

LYZBET. I don't want to.

BEAUTY. There are times in this life we must accept a path that's not of our own choosing. You will go. And, in time, you'll understand it's what's best.

LYZBET. What of the land? What of my home?

BEAUTY. I intend to hold it in trust until such a time as you've completed your studies and the proceeds of any sale will be made available to you. By such time I don't doubt you'll be able to put such proceeds to good use. And when the time's right, you'll make someone a fine bride – this wealth will assist that to no end.

LYZBET. I'm sure I have no more interest in acquiring a husband than you do, Mr. Smith.

*(The door opens and **CURLY** enters.)*

CURLY. What's goin' on? What are you doin' here?

BEAUTY. My name is Beauty Smith.

CURLY. I know who you are.

BEAUTY. And I'm simply having a rational discussion with Miss Scott. So I'll thank you not to become excited on her behalf.

CURLY. She's told me all about you. And she's made it clear you ain't welcome here.

BEAUTY. Such confrontations are a thing of the past. Isn't that right, Lyzbet.

CURLY. I think it's about time you left, Mr. Smith.

BEAUTY. Of course. The girl needs her rest. I'll return within the week and we shall make the arrangements.

CURLY. For what? Arrangements for what?

BEAUTY. You know, Lyzbet, your grandfather was a good man. I knew him for many years and there wasn't many a man finer. The day of your family's demise, your grandfather showed his true spirit when he lowered his rifle and spared your life. He gave you a chance to live, and now, in that vein, we're giving you the chance to live that life better.

LYZBET. What d'you mean? Lowered his rifle?

BEAUTY. Well, isn't that the mark of a true Christian? For a man with no sin in his life, he has nothin' to repent. But for a man to commit sin, and in the very midst of that sin to find redemption with such an act of compassion – well, that's surely the path to somewhere better.

LYZBET. What sin?

(Silence.)

BEAUTY. He never told you?

LYZBET. Told me what?

BEAUTY. You believe Weedon Scott simply stumbled upon you in the middle of that massacre? That he serendipitously arrived mere moments after the hunters withdrew?

(She doesn't respond.)

Forgive me, Lyzbet, I had assumed you knew the truth of the matter.

LYZBET. What truth? Say it plainly.

CURLY. Don't listen to this, Elizabeth. Don't listen to a word this man says.

BEAUTY. Weedon Scott didn't arrive once the hunters withdrew. Weedon Scott was one of the hunters. And he slew the natives of that tribe without remorse – until his eyes fell on you.

LYZBET. That can't be true...

CURLY. It isn't.

BEAUTY. Forgive me, Lyzbet, I had assumed he'd told you such. I'm sure, given time, he would have done.

(Silence.)

Think carefully about what we've discussed here, Miss Scott. Don't dwell in the past. Look to the future. Think about what the future will offer you. I'll return within the week.

(**BEAUTY** *leaves.*)

CURLY. You don't believe him?

LYZBET. There's no use in you comin' by here. I don't need your lookin' after me.

CURLY. What arrangements was he talkin' about?

LYZBET. I'm gonna be goin' away for a time.

CURLY. How long a time?

LYZBET. Maybe for good.

CURLY. What are you talkin' about? Goin' where?

LYZBET. A school. They've made arrangements.

CURLY. Who's they? Why are you lettin' people make arrangements on your behalf?

LYZBET. I'm on the register with the Department of Indian Affairs. You have a complaint? Make it with them.

CURLY. They want to send you to a residential school and you're goin' willingly?

LYZBET. I'm not goin' willingly. I'm just not fightin' anymore.

CURLY. You know what they do in them schools?

LYZBET. I know no more than you do.

CURLY. Well I know plenty. I heard kids die in there. They die, and no one even notices. The school buries 'em in unmarked graves. And they're gone. Vanished and disappeared and gone. Forgotten. That what you want? To be forgotten? Left to rot in an unmarked grave?

(Silence.)

If you're lucky, and you survive the years, they're still gonna wash away every last bit of the In'jun from you. Wash away every last bit of who you are till you're just another conquered native.

LYZBET. Well perhaps that's better.

CURLY. Better'n what?

LYZBET. Better than havin' a foot in each world and bein' an outsider in both. I'm not In'jun – I've been playin'

Elizabeth Maria Scott so long the native's already been washed away. Maybe, I go to this school, they finish what's begun. Then all anyone will see is a girl – just the same as any other.

CURLY. No white person will ever see you the same as them. That's God's honest truth. You will always be different and they will never accept you as one of their own.

LYZBET. Why not? You have.

CURLY. No I haven't. I've accepted you for who and what you are. Because who and what you are is a gift, Elizabeth – it's a gift given to you, and it's a gift given to anyone who crosses your path. You are a gift to me – can't you see that?

(Silence.)

LYZBET. I'd like you to leave.

CURLY. Don't you dare let that man's words get inside your mind. Don't let that poison in.

LYZBET. I'm done fightin'. Can't you understand that? I've been fightin' my whole life to be somethin' I'm not. I fought with words. I've fought with a blade. I spilled blood. And look what I have to show for it. My family is dead and I have nothin' left to fight for.

CURLY. Nothin'?

LYZBET. Curly – go.

(Silence.)

Please.

*(**CURLY** moves to the door.)*

CURLY. There's a life in you I seen from the moment we met. Even if you got nothin' else, fight for *that*. 'Cause that is somethin' worth fightin' for.

*(**CURLY** leaves.)*

COMPANY.
WE PARTED OUR WAYS AT THE FIRST FALL OF SNOW,
FOR THE WARM SUNNY SOUTH YOU WERE BOUND,

YOU PROMISED BY SPRING YOU'D RETURN WITH MY HEART.
BUT THE FROST STILL LIES DEEP ON THE GROUND.

OH THE TEARDROPS ARE FALLIN' SINCE YOU'VE LEFT ME,
YES THE TEARDROPS HAVE FALLEN SINCE YOU'VE GONE,
BUT THE SNOW CATCHES EACH TUMBLIN' MOMENT,
AND TO ICE EVERY SORROW'S NOW BECOME.

I'VE HOPE IN MY HEART AS THE DAYS COME AND GO,
BUT THE DAYS TURN TO WEEKS AND MONTHS TO YEARS,
WILL THE WARMTH OF YOUR LOVE COME MELT ALL THE SNOW?
OR WILL I DROWN IN A VALE OF FROZEN TEARS?

OH THE TEARDROPS ARE FALLIN' SINCE YOU'VE LEFT ME,
YES THE TEARDROPS HAVE FALLEN SINCE YOU'VE GONE,
BUT THE SNOW CATCHES EACH TUMBLIN' MOMENT,
AND TO ICE EVERY SORROW'S NOW BECOME.

Scene Six: The Illusion Of It

> (**LYZBET** *is packing a trunk with clothes and other items. She is dressed in the clothes in which Weedon had wrapped her as a child.*)
>
> (*A knock comes at the door.*)
>
> (**CURLY** *opens the door and steps inside.*)

LYZBET. Since when did you knock?

CURLY. Since I thought maybe we weren't friends no longer.

LYZBET. I didn't take you to be the kind to feel emotions over strong words.

CURLY. Likewise.

LYZBET. Shall we agree we're each forgiven for whatever might have been said between us?

CURLY. Agreed. Though I fear you benefit greater from that deal.

LYZBET. I thought you said "agreed"?

CURLY. Alright. Agreed. I won't say another word.

> (*Silence.*)

I ain't never seen you dressed like that.

LYZBET. That's 'cause I haven't.

CURLY. Well you look like an authentic squaw to me.

> (*Silence.*)

I brought you this. A partin' gift.

> (*Silence.*)

It ain't much really. I couldn't think what they'd let you keep so I figured somethin' small. Somethin' that wouldn't cause offense.

> (**CURLY** *passes her a piece of leather with a drawing marked on it.*)

It's a drawin'.

LYZBET. I can see it's a drawin'.

CURLY. It's meant to be the sun settin' over the mountains.

LYZBET. Did you draw it?

CURLY. I did.

LYZBET. It ain't a great likeness.

CURLY. I ain't never claimed to be an artist. Just figured so you have somethin' – no matter how far away you go – somethin' to make sure you don't never forget.

LYZBET. I'm never goin' to forget.

CURLY. Pretty sure that's the full intention of them schools. This way, you got somethin' you can carry with you – always.

(Silence.)

LYZBET. Beauty Smith's gonna be here soon to accompany me to Dawson.

CURLY. Alright.

(Silence.)

LYZBET. I'm not one for farewells.

CURLY. Alright.

(Silence.)

LYZBET. Well alright then.

*(**LYZBET** continues to pack her things.)*

*(**CURLY** moves to the door, but it bursts open and **TOM** enters.)*

TOM. Lyzbet!

LYZBET. What are you doin' here?

TOM. I had to see you.

LYZBET. On account of what? Why aren't you out for the caribou?

TOM. I was. We was huntin' out near Eden's Croft when the news came.

CURLY. What news?

TOM. They found Jim Hall...alive.

LYZBET. I cut his throat and waited till the blood run dry. There's no way he woke from that.

TOM. They captured him near three weeks back hidin' in a cabin in Eastern Nebraska. Word only just reached us.

LYZBET. That's not possible. I've hunted enough to know when a creature's dead. I felt the life go from him.

TOM. Don't you understand? I ain't sayin' you didn't kill a man. I ain't sayin' you didn't kill the fella that murdered Weedon.

CURLY. Then what are you sayin'?

TOM. That Weedon's killer weren't Jim Hall.

CURLY. So he weren't Jim Hall. What does it matter?

LYZBET. It matters because somebody wanted us to *think* it was Jim Hall.

TOM. I've been thinkin' it over and again, right the way here.

LYZBET. He came to find you in town. He fabricated the entire story.

CURLY. Who did?

LYZBET. The only man who's ever wanted somethin' from us. The same man who's about to come remove me from this land. He murdered my grandfather, and he wanted us to believe it was Jim Hall.

TOM. I figure the fella you left out there for the wolves – I figure him to be that Griffith fella.

LYZBET. He was here, that night the four of you were drinkin'. He was here.

TOM. You didn't recognize him out there?

LYZBET. I wasn't lookin' to. I was only lookin' for vengeance. I thought I'd found it.

TOM. I figure Beauty never anticipated you catchin' his man.

CURLY. I guess he underestimated you.

LYZBET. More than he knows.

CURLY. So what do we do now? We go to town? We go to the law?

LYZBET. Is that the right thing?

CURLY. Tom?

TOM. He was your grandfather. I reckon that makes it your decision.

LYZBET. Then I'm not goin' to the law. And if you two are afraid of meeting the inside of a cell, or the dealin' end of a rope, you best make yourselves scarce from this land and find somewhere with plenty of options for an alibi.

CURLY. You can't do this alone.

LYZBET. I can. Because just like you said, the man underestimates me. He thinks I'm just a little girl, but I'm not. I'm a hunter. And this is just like any other hunt. I have all the time in the universe. And Beauty Smith, well, Beauty Smith only has the *illusion* of it.

*(**LYZBET** collects a bowl and pulls leaves and seeds from her pack. She grinds them together, creating a thick black paste. Coating her fingers in the dark paint, she draws it across her face, marking each cheek.)*

NARRATION. The wolf now slept, but lived yet in her blood aside the noble warriors of her past, and gifted her the strength in hour of need, to guide her hand and stead'ly sure her bolt, that arrow through the air might make its mark upon the vicious life that wished hers dead. Her forebears' magic soared to make her strong, and through the years they called their ancient song.

Scene Seven: The Blood Of Two Lives

(In the Northland Wild, **BEAUTY SMITH** *walks cautiously forward. He surveys the landscape.)*

BEAUTY. Lyzbet?

(No answer.)

We don't have time for games, Miss Scott. I discovered your note – this is not what we agreed.

(No answer.)

We arranged to meet at your grandfather's home. I find no amusement in your dragging me all the way out here. So come on out.

(Silence.)

Show yourself.

(In the distance, a wolf howls.)

I am not amused, Miss Scott.

(Another wolf howls, but closer and in the opposite direction. **BEAUTY** *draws his pistol.)*

(The howls come from all directions. **BEAUTY** *readies himself. He is visibly panicked.)*

You show yourself now, Lyzbet, or I'll be forced to return with the authorities. You understand? Lyzbet?

(The pack is closing in. The howls are louder and louder until –)

(The sound of the air being split in two.)

*(***BEAUTY*** emits a terrible scream and falls to the ground, his gun dropping from his hand – an arrow has pierced his thigh.)*

Jesus Christ!

*(***LYZBET*** is on him. In her hands, bow and arrow poised to deliver a fatal strike.)*

LYZBET. Reach for that gun and the next arrow will find its way right to your heart.

BEAUTY. You stupid little girl! What in the hell have you done?

LYZBET. Don't excite yourself, Mr. Smith. It won't do you any favors.

BEAUTY. Lyzbet… Listen to me… Help me down off this mountain, get me to the physician, and I won't have charges brought against you. This will simply be an accident – a hunting accident. Nothing more. You understand?

(A wolf howls in the distance.)

LYZBET. The pack's huntin', Mr. Smith. Won't be long till they scent your blood on the air.

BEAUTY. Do you have any idea the trouble you're going to be in?

LYZBET. Somewhat less than you're in right this moment.

BEAUTY. You know what I can have done to you? You know what I can do to you?

LYZBET. The same thing you did to my grandfather?

BEAUTY. I don't know what you're talking about.

LYZBET. They buried him up on that ridge long before he should have been in the ground. He was murdered, without a chance to say goodbye, to make his peace – without a chance for forgiveness.

BEAUTY. I had nothin' to do with Weedon's death.

LYZBET. So you know what I'm accusin' you of?

BEAUTY. This is preposterous.

*(**LYZBET** collects **BEAUTY**'s pistol.)*

LYZBET. They found Jim Hall.

BEAUTY. They found him? Good.

LYZBET. Only it wasn't in the place I left my grandfather's killer. Jim Hall's alive and well and whatever he might be guilty of, when it comes to the murder of Weedon Scott, he's innocent.

BEAUTY. How can you know that?

LYZBET. Jim Hall was captured over two thousand miles from here, right about the time my grandfather was killed.

BEAUTY. So Jim Hall's innocent? His innocence doesn't mean my guilt.

LYZBET. You played a role in my grandfather's death. We both know that to be a fact.

BEAUTY. You believe it to be a fact? Then take me into Dawson. Hand me over to the authorities and give them the opportunity to prove it.

LYZBET. I've no intention of doin' that.

BEAUTY. I'll stand trial, if that's what you want? I'll stand trial for what you're accusing me of.

LYZBET. No, you won't.

BEAUTY. You intend to kill me? Is that it? You want justice?

LYZBET. I want retribution.

BEAUTY. You won't find it in murdering me. Lyzbet, I've been good to you – I've tried to find a new life for you.

LYZBET. You'd have sent me to that school and you'd have murdered all that's remainin' of Lyzbet Scott. Then you'd have the blood of two lives on your hands. I won't give you the chance for that.

BEAUTY. You're not going to kill me, Lyzbet. Search inside yourself, you're a hunter, that's right, but you're not a murderer. You'd kill to defend yourself, what you love. That's noble. But you're not going to murder an unarmed man – in cold blood. I know that. We both do. You're not going to deliver the fatal blow.

LYZBET. I already have.

BEAUTY. No, you haven't. This arrow was an act of emotion – I understand that, and I can forgive it. It doesn't have to mean death.

LYZBET. I didn't mean that poetically, Mr. Smith. I mean that arrow's coated with baneroot. The time we've been talkin', it's for certain in your veins. When your sight begins to depart, that's when it's takin' hold. It won't be long before all your senses fail you. Pretty soon after that, it'll be your organs takin' a permanent leave. So you see, Mr. Beauty Smith, you're just about the healthiest dead man I've ever laid eyes on.

(Silence.)

*(**BEAUTY** starts to slowly laugh.)*

I can't figure what you could find amusin'.

BEAUTY. You think killing me's gonna be the end of your troubles? It's only going to be the beginning. There are men out there far worse than me. Men who'll come for the gold in this mountain and won't think twice about putting a bullet between your eyes.

LYZBET. Is that so?

BEAUTY. I'm a saint next to those men. You understand? You think you can get rid of me and have your life back the way it was? Your life is about to become a fresh nightmare of hell. The law will come for you. You know that? And the law won't blink before it hangs a native little bitch. You'll be begging for your life just like your dear old grandpa was. Soiling your loins with fear. Weeping like a babe thrown to the wolves. You want retribution? Well it's goddamn coming for you.

(His words have begun to slur. His eyes dart rapidly.)

Your grandfather was weak. He was a weak, savage-loving coward.

LYZBET. There are many ill things you could say of my grandfather. More'n half of them would most likely be true. But the one thing he wasn't, was a coward.

(His words are slurring as his head begins to loll.)

BEAUTY. I'm gonna hunt you down, girl. I'm gonna find you and fill your remaining hours with the worst suffering on this earth. Believe that. I will find you.

LYZBET. The sun's goin' down so fast on you, Beauty Smith, I doubt you could find your own ass.

BEAUTY. You're gonna pay for this. You're gonna pay tenfold.

LYZBET. That may be. But it won't be you collectin' the debt.

(She turns to leave.)

BEAUTY. Wait! Lyzbet! I have money. I have coin. It's yours. Get me to the physician.

LYZBET. If I were you, I'd pray that baneroot takes hold before the pack finds you.

*(**LYZBET** is leaving.)*

BEAUTY. I'll make you rich. I'll make you rich, Lyzbet, and you won't ever have to see me again.

(Silence.)

Don't leave me here!

(Silence.)

Lyzbet…

(Silence.)

I'll kill you! You hear me? I'll kill you!

COMPANY.
>MY HOMELAND'S CALLING.
>MY HEART IS TORN.
>AND ALL I LONG FOR,
>IS ONCE MORE,
>
>TO SEE MY COUNTRY,
>WHERE MY HOME LIES,
>ACROSS THE WATERS,
>BEYOND THE SKIES.
>
>MY HOMELAND'S CALLING.
>MY HEART IS TORN.
>AND ALL I LONG FOR,
>IS ONCE MORE,
>
>TO SEE MY FAMILY,
>TO CROSS THE HEARTH,

OF MY KIN'S HOMESTEAD,
TO BURY MY HEART.

MY HOMELAND'S CALLING.
MY HEART IS TORN.
AND ALL I LONG FOR,
FOREVER MORE,

TO MEET REDEMPTION,
WHERE I WAS BORN.
MY HOMELAND'S CALLING.
MY HEART IS TORN.

Scene Eight: A Good Name

(**LYZBET** *is preparing a canoe by the river.* **CURLY** *approaches.*)

CURLY. I know you ain't fond of farewells, but I weren't about to let you leave without sayin' my own.

LYZBET. How'd you find me?

CURLY. Didn't I ever tell you? This land is my home, just the same as yours.

(*Silence.*)

They're talkin' 'bout Beauty in town. Heard some hunters found him up there – what was left of him.

LYZBET. They suspect foul play?

CURLY. I guess so. Difficult to blame natural causes when there's an arrow stickin' out his ass.

(*Silence.*)

Where d'you intend to go? The law's gonna hunt you. You're aware of that, right?

LYZBET. I'm aware. And they're more than welcome to try. I'll travel downriver till I reach the Klondike. I'll stay with her till there's miles enough behind me. They'll have a difficult time followin' tracks across water.

CURLY. And where d'you go from there?

LYZBET. I'm not sure. I'll head beyond the mountains. I heard once there's a whole world of danger and excitement out there – just waitin' to be discovered.

CURLY. I guess I don't have much right to feel it, nor to say it, but it breaks my heart to think of you alone out there.

LYZBET. I won't be alone. I won't ever be alone. This is my land, the land of my people – so long as I walk this land, they'll be with me. And who knows, maybe in time I'll find them – find what's left of them.

CURLY. I wish I could come with you.

LYZBET. You've got a life here, Curly. A good life. You've no cause to throw that away on account of me.

CURLY. I would, if you asked, I'd come with you.

LYZBET. Why would you do somethin' like that?

CURLY. Ain't it obvious?

(Silence.)

There's a whole world of danger and excitement out there. Just like you said. And I'd come discover it with you, if you asked.

LYZBET. I'm not askin'. And I won't ask.

CURLY. I've never met no one like you before, Elizabeth.

LYZBET. Well I guess you can count yourself lucky for that.

CURLY. I know most of what the man said was lies, but what Beauty told you about Weedon...

LYZBET. There's dark and light inside all of us. My grandfather wasn't any different. Whatever he may have done in his life, he also saved mine. I ought to be grateful for that. I *am* grateful for that.

(Silence.)

I'll miss this land, Curly. I'll miss this land, the mountains, the river, and I'll miss you.

CURLY. Maybe one day, when time's passed enough, you could return.

LYZBET. Maybe. One day.

CURLY. There'll soon be a reward out. If anyone asks, wherever it is you're goin', you oughtn't give 'em your real name.

LYZBET. Elizabeth Maria was the girl who lived in these parts with Old Man Scott. That life's over. That girl's gone. So it makes sense the name goes with her.

CURLY. You figured what you'll call yourself? So I can listen out if I ever hear stories of your adventures.

LYZBET. I thought, maybe...Wâpamîpita.

CURLY. That's a good name. White Fang – the strongest creature I ever knew.

LYZBET. In the language of my people, there is no word for "goodbye." Only "kîhtwâm ka-wâpamitin."

CURLY. What does it mean?

LYZBET. I'll see you again.

CURLY. Kîhtwâm ka-wâpamitin.

(CURLY kisses LYZBET on the cheek.)

LYZBET. You were right, Curly. Whatever darkness may come, this life – it's well worth fightin' for.

(She kisses CURLY. LYZBET climbs into the canoe and pushes off down the river.)

I've heard a story, whispered in the night, when grey of day has faded into dark and pall of Arctic black has fallen fast. Beneath the spirits' green and swirling light, a girl who gazed within the fire's flame and witnessed there a vision in the smoke – a life without the pack but not alone, for beating true, a heart now of my own.

The End

CREE GLOSSARY

Instructions:

Sit	*koskwâtapi*
Stay	*kisata*
Wait	*pêtâ*
No	*namoya / nama*
Go	*niyâ*
Go home	*kiwe*
Go away	*sipwêtê*
Go away right now	*sêmâk sipwêtê*
Go outside	*wayawi*
Go hunting	*machi*
Come here	*âstam*
Be careful	*awahê*
Eat it	*michi*

Questions:

What is it?	*keko*
What is the matter?	*tânêhki*

Greetings:

I'll see you again	*kîhtwâm ka-wâpamitin*

Other:

White Teeth	*wâpamîpita*
My friend	*nichewakan*
Son of a bitch	*kiskânak kosisan*

www.ingramcontent.com/pod-product-compliance
Lightning Source LLC
Chambersburg PA
CBHW051409290426
44108CB00015B/2222